Bible Puzzles for Children

VOLUME 3

Words of Jesus

by Ruby A. Maschke

Judson Press® Valley Forge

Table of Contents

Bible References

Words of Jesus in Prayer

Words of Jesus in Teaching

Words of Jesus in Healing

Words of Jesus in Miracles

Words of Jesus in Parables

Words of Jesus in Blessings

Introduction

Children enjoy the challenge of puzzles. They also enjoy hearing stories about improbable things such as putting back a man's ear after it was cut off—or telling a storm to stop. When the puzzles and stories are combined, children learn about Jesus.

One puzzle can help children learn the Lord's Prayer, the perfect prayer. Other puzzles tell children that Jesus was always willing to talk about faith to crowds or to just one person. He helped people by healing blindness and by feeding thousands. He taught stories, called parables, using earthly examples such as treasure and neighbors.

After teaching Sunday school for many years, I wanted to tell Bible stories to even more children. It is my hope and prayer that every child who works these puzzles will know that Jesus can do anything and that he is always with them and loves them very much—so much that he died on the cross and three days later rose again, which was the greatest miracle of all. He did it for everyone!

Learning can be fun. Learning about Jesus can be joyful. To the child who solves these puzzles, let there be not just the joy of learning, but the joy of Jesus in your heart!

Ruby A. Maschke

Words of Jesus ...

In Prayer

Jesus said, "Therefore I tell you,
whatever you ask for in prayer,
believe that you have received it,
and it will be yours."

(Mark 11:24)

Where? When? Why? How?

To read some things Jesus said about prayer, fill in the blanks by changing the letters, using the following code: A=B, B=C, C=D, etc.

1. WHERE should we pray?

When you pray, go into your <u>r</u> <u>o</u> <u>o</u> <u>m</u>, <u>c</u> <u>l</u> <u>o</u> <u>s</u> <u>e</u>
                                           Q N N L B K N R D

the <u>d</u> <u>o</u> <u>o</u> <u>r</u> and pray to your <u>F</u> A <u>t</u> <u>h</u> <u>e</u> <u>r</u>,
       C N N Q   E   S G D Q

who is unseen. Then your <u>F</u> A <u>t</u> <u>h</u> <u>e</u> <u>r</u> . . . will
                                 E   S G D Q

<u>r</u> <u>e</u> <u>w</u> A <u>r</u> <u>d</u> you. (Matthew 6:6)
Q D V   Q C

2. WHEN should we pray?

Jesus <u>t</u> <u>o</u> <u>l</u> <u>d</u> his <u>d</u> <u>i</u> <u>s</u> <u>c</u> <u>i</u> <u>p</u> <u>l</u> <u>e</u> <u>s</u>
       S N K C   C H R B H O K D R

. . . that <u>t</u> <u>h</u> <u>e</u> <u>y</u> <u>s</u> <u>h</u> <u>o</u> <u>u</u> <u>l</u> <u>d</u>
         S G D X   R G N T K C

A <u>l</u> <u>y</u>. A <u>b</u> <u>s</u> pray and not <u>g</u> <u>i</u> <u>v</u> <u>e</u>
  K V   X R   F H U D

<u>u</u> <u>s</u>. (Luke 18:1)
T O

3. WHY should we pray?

W A <u>t</u> <u>c</u> <u>h</u> and pray so that you <u>W</u> <u>i</u> <u>l</u> <u>l</u>
V   S   B   G   V   H   K   K

not <u>f</u> A <u>l</u> <u>l</u> into
    E   K   K

<u>t</u> <u>e</u> <u>m</u> <u>p</u> <u>t</u> A <u>t</u> <u>i</u> <u>o</u> <u>n</u>.
S D L O S   S H N M

The <u>S</u> <u>p</u> <u>i</u> <u>r</u> <u>i</u> <u>t</u> is <u>w</u> <u>i</u> <u>l</u> <u>l</u> <u>i</u> <u>n</u> <u>g</u>,
    R O H Q H S   V H K K H M F

but the <u>b</u> <u>o</u> <u>d</u> <u>y</u> is <u>w</u> <u>e</u> A <u>h</u>. (Matthew 26:41)
        A N C X   V D   J

4. HOW should we pray?

I will do <u>W</u> <u>h</u> A __ __ __ __ __
        V G   S D U D Q

you ask in my __ A __ __, so that the Son may
               M   L D

__ __ __ __ __ __ __ __ __ __ to the
A Q H M F   F K N Q X

__ A __ __ __ __. You may A __ __ me for
E   S G D Q   R J

A __ __ __ __ __ __ __ in my __ A __ __,
  M X S G H M F   M   L D

and I __ __ __ __ do it. (John 14:13-14)
      V H K K

9

A Perfect Prayer

Jesus said, "This, then, is how you should pray."
    Fit the words in the list into the blank squares, then place them into the prayer, matching the numbers. Memorize the prayer, so that you can pray it every night when you go to bed. (Matthew 6:9-13)

also	evil	give	today
come	Father	hallowed	will
deliver	forgive	heaven	
earth	from	name	

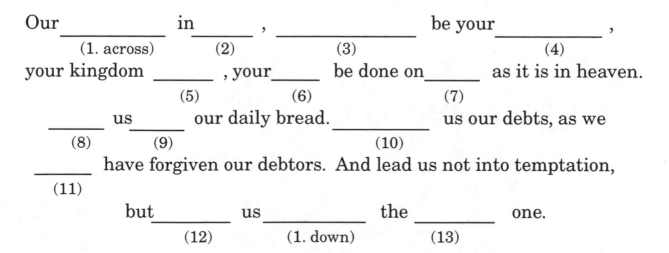

Our _____ in _____ , _____ be your _____ ,
     (1. across)   (2)   (3)   (4)
your kingdom _____ , your _____ be done on _____ as it is in heaven.
     (5)   (6)   (7)
_____ us _____ our daily bread. _____ us our debts, as we
     (8)   (9)   (10)
_____ have forgiven our debtors. And lead us not into temptation,
     (11)
but _____ us _____ the _____ one.
     (12)   (1. down)   (13)

A Powerful Prayer

A friend of Jesus named Lazarus died and was buried in a tomb in a cave, with a stone at the entrance. Jesus went to the tomb and said, "Take away the stone." So they took it away, and Jesus prayed, "Father, I thank you that you have heard me. I knew that you always hear me, but I said this for the benefit of the people standing here, that they may believe that you sent me."

Then Jesus called, "Lazarus, come out!" And Lazarus came out of the tomb, alive again. (John 11:14-44)

Find the words from the story in the puzzle square. Words may be up or down, across or diagonal, backward or forward.

always	have	Lazarus	thank
believe	hear	people	that
benefit	heard	said	they
come	here	sent	this
Father	knew	standing	

```
C  B  E  L  I  E  V  E  M  D
P  E  O  P  L  E  N  E  P  F
Q  N  G  R  H  S  I  S  T  J
H  E  A  R  U  T  H  E  Y  L
E  F  A  T  H  E  R  N  K  A
R  I  V  A  E  L  W  T  M  Z
E  T  N  H  A  V  E  X  N  A
Y  K  T  O  R  L  Z  T  A  R
M  N  B  H  D  N  W  H  C  U
O  E  G  N  I  D  N  A  T  S
D  W  P  E  Q  S  F  T  Y  R
G  E  M  O  C  S  D  I  A  S
```

A Prayer about Eternal Life

When Jesus knew the Roman soldiers were going to arrest him, he prayed to his heavenly Father. To read part of his prayer, place the words in the hands into the sentences, matching the numbers. (John 17:1-5)

1._____has come. 2._____,
that your Son may glorify you. For you 3._____
4._____ that he might 5._____
to all those you 6._____.
Now this 7._____: that they may know you,
8. _____, and Jesus Christ,
whom you have sent. I have 9._____
on earth by 10._____ you gave me to do.
And now, Father, glorify me 11._____
with the glory I had with you 12._____began.

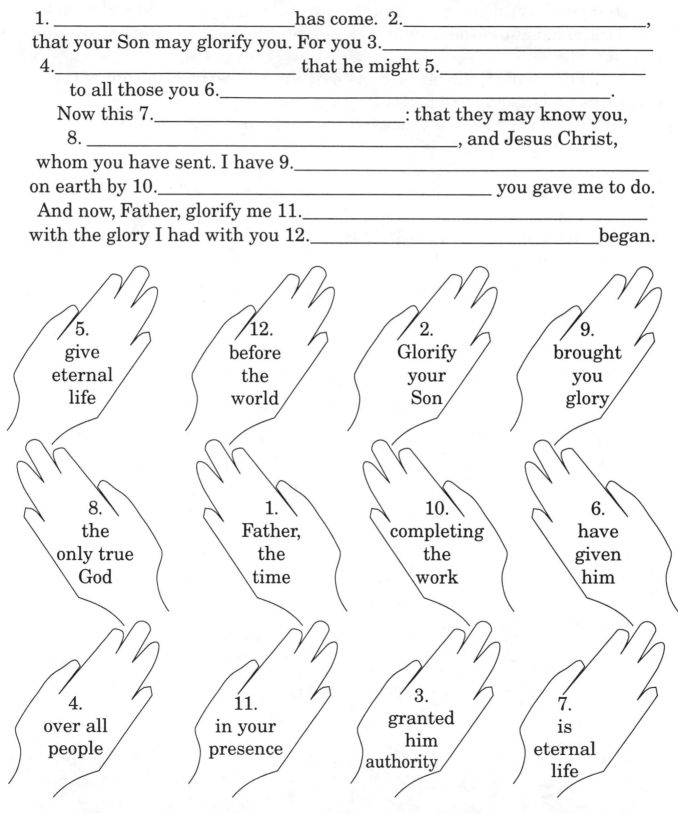

12

A Prayer in a Garden

Jesus went to a special place in the Garden of Gethsemane to pray. That place was called the Mount of Olives. There he said to his disciples, "Pray that you will not fall into temptation." He went a short distance, knelt down and prayed, "Father, if you are willing, take this cup from me; yet not my will, but yours be done." An angel from heaven appeared to him and strengthened him. (Luke 22:39-43)

Find the way through the maze from the disciples to Jesus and the angel.

A Prayer for Roman Soldiers

When Jesus was crucified (nailed to the cross), he prayed for the soldiers who were so cruel. To read his prayer, write a definition for each word in the word list. Place the letters in the blanks in the cross, matching the numbers, to read Jesus' prayer. (Luke 23:34)

a. We eat _____   ___ ___ ___ ___
                                18 28 46 25

b. At no time   ___ ___ ___ ___ ___
                   31 5 12 40 43

c. 3 times 10   ___ ___ ___ ___ ___ ___
                  3 15 47 20 37 24

d. Used to make flour   ___ ___ ___ ___ ___
                   33 22 44 36 29

e. Rise from sleep   ___ ___ ___ ___
                 34 2 30 13

f. Singular of teeth   ___ ___ ___ ___ ___
                 14 8 26 38 4

g. Stars shine at _____   ___ ___ ___ ___ ___
                           48 11 49 35 21

h. _____, set, go!   ___ ___ ___ ___ ___
                         6 16 42 45 41

i. Shape   ___ ___ ___ ___
                 1 32 9 17

j. It lays eggs   ___ ___ ___
                39 23 27

k. Moisture in air   ___ ___ ___
                7 19 10

___ ___ ___ ___ ___ ___ ,
 1 2 3 4 5 6

___ ___ ___ ___ ___ ___ ___
 7 8 9 10 11 12 13

___ ___ ___ ___ ,   ___ ___ ___
 14 15 16 17   18 19 20

___ ___ ___ ___   ___ ___   ___ ___ ___
 21 22 23 24   25 26   27 28 29

___ ___ ___ ___
 30 31 32 33

___ ___ ___ ___
 34 35 36 37

___ ___ ___ ___
 38 39 40 41

___ ___ ___
 42 43 44

___ ___ ___ ___ ___ .
 45 46 47 48 49

Words of Jesus ...

In Teaching

Some men said to Jesus, "Teacher, we know you are a man of integrity. . . . you teach the way of God in accordance with the truth." (Mark 12:14)

Where? Telling What? Doing What?

Where did Jesus teach? What did he tell people? What else did he do?
Use the code to find the answers to those questions. (Matthew 4:23)

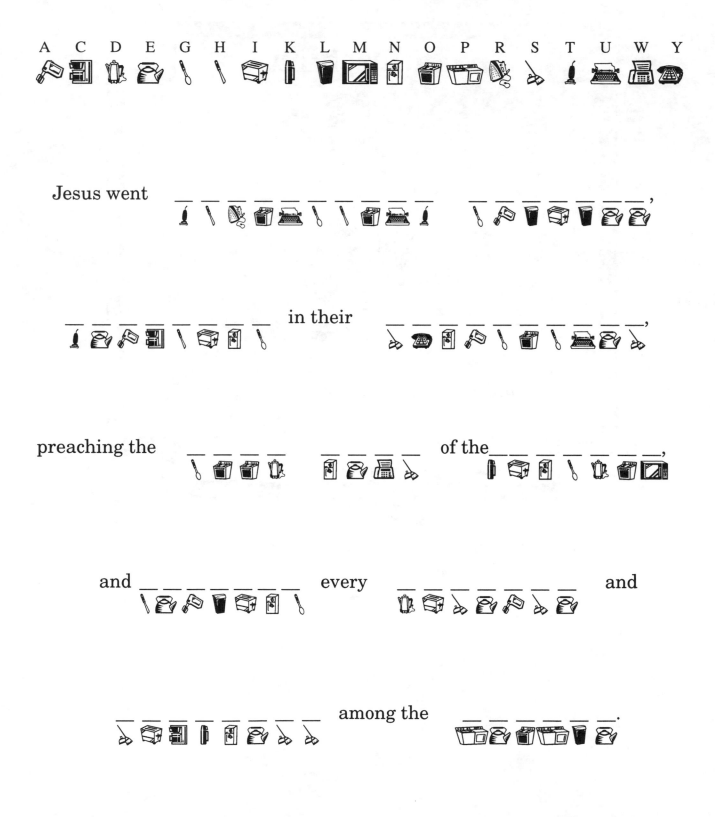

16

To Crowds of People

When <u>Jesus</u> had <u>finished</u> <u>saying</u> <u>these</u> <u>things</u>, the <u>crowds</u> <u>were</u> <u>amazed</u> at his <u>teaching</u>, <u>because</u> he <u>taught</u> as one who had <u>authority</u>, and not as <u>their</u> <u>teachers</u> of the law. (Matthew 7:28-29)

Fit the underlined words into the blank squares. Some letters have been filled in to give you clues.

About Sheep and Shepherds

When Jesus saw a large crowd, he had compassion on them because they were like sheep without a shepherd. So he began teaching them many things. (Mark 6:34) Another time he told people something that you can read when you work the puzzle. (John 10:11) Be sure to add or subtract the letters, following directions.

Jesus said, " 

— O L  — L P

______ ______

the good  — E +  — A T + D,

______ ______

The good shepherd  — D B U G + S

______

down his 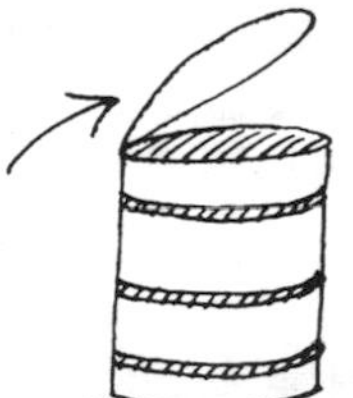 — D +  — I V

______ ______

for the  — L L + E +  — I N.

______ ______

To Nicodemus

    A man named Nicodemus was a member of the Jewish ruling council. He came to Jesus one night to ask how he could have eternal life. Jesus taught Nicodemus what is sometimes called "the Gospel in a nutshell." To find what Jesus said, write all of the letters in the number "1" squares, then all of the letters in the number "2" squares and so on. (John 3:16)

1 F	2 E	3 H	4 S	5 Y	6 O	7 V	8 A	9 S	10 T	1 O
2 D	3 A	4 O	5 S	6 E	7 E	8 L	9 H	10 E	1 R	2 T
3 T	4 N	5 O	6 V	7 S	8 L	9 B	10 R	1 G	2 H	3 H
4 E	5 N	6 E	7 I	8 N	9 U	10 N	1 O	2 E	3 E	4 A
5 T	6 R	7 N	8 O					9 T	10 A	1 D
2 W	3 G	4 N	5 H					6 B	7 H	8 T
9 H	10 L	1 S	2 O					3 A	4 D	5 A
6 E	7 I	8 P	9 A					10 L	1 O	2 R
3 V	4 O	5 T	6 L	7 M	8 E	9 V	10 I	1 L	2 L	3 E
4 N	5 W	6 I	7 S	8 R	9 E	10 F	1 O	2 D	3 H	4 L
	5 H	6 E	7 H	8 I	9 E	10 E	1 V	2 T	3 I	

_____

_____

_____

To His Disciples

Before Jesus ascended to heaven, he gave his disciples a special message. To read that message, place the letters into the blank spaces, matching the numbers. (Matthew 28:18-20)

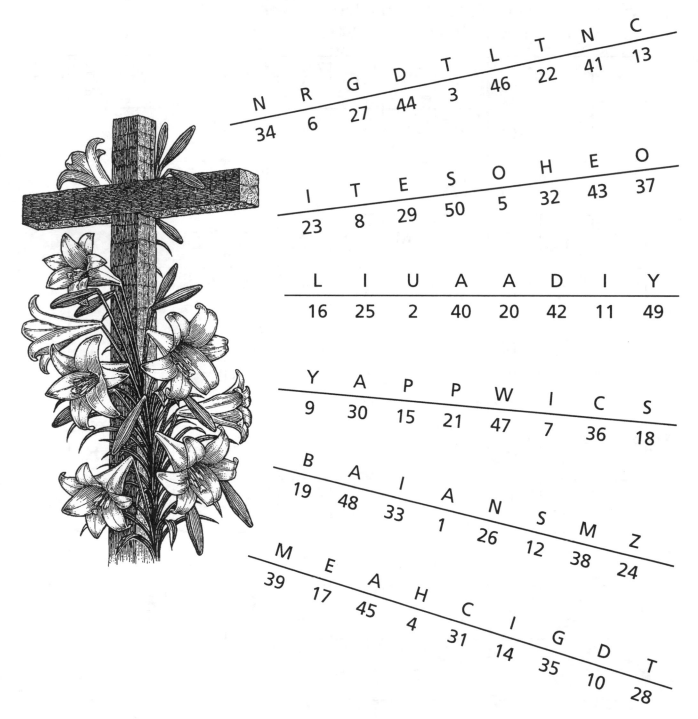

Then Jesus came to them and said, "All $\underline{}\ \underline{}\ \underline{}\ \underline{}\ \underline{}\ \underline{}\ \underline{}\ \underline{}\ \underline{}$
                                                          1 2 3 4 5 6 7 8 9

in heaven and on earth has been given to me. Therefore

go and make $\underline{}\ \underline{}\ \underline{}\ \underline{}\ \underline{}\ \underline{}\ \underline{}\ \underline{}\ \underline{}$ of all
                         10 11 12 13 14 15 16 17 18

nations, $\underline{}\ \underline{}\ \underline{}\ \underline{}\ \underline{}\ \underline{}\ \underline{}\ \underline{}\ \underline{}$ them in the name
               19 20 21 22 23 24 25 26 27

of the Father and of the Son and of the Holy Spirit,

and $\underline{}\ \underline{}\ \underline{}\ \underline{}\ \underline{}\ \underline{}\ \underline{}\ \underline{}$ them to obey everything I have
          28 29 30 31 32 33 34 35

$\underline{}\ \underline{}\ \underline{}\ \underline{}\ \underline{}\ \underline{}\ \underline{}\ \underline{}\ \underline{}$ you. And surely I will be
36 37 38 39 40 41 42 43 44

with you $\underline{}\ \underline{}\ \underline{}\ \underline{}\ \underline{}\ \underline{}$,   to the very end of the age."
              45 46 47 48 49 50

At the Tabernacle

Once Jesus went to a meal called The Feast of Tabernacles. A tabernacle was a place of worship, and the Bible says that Jesus went to the tabernacle courts and began to teach. The Jews asked, "How did this man get such learning without having studied?" To find Jesus' answer, work the crossword puzzle, then write the words into the sentence, using the numbers that are in the puzzle. (John 7:16-17)

Across
3. No way!
4. Opposite of toward
6. Which one?
7. Mailed a letter
9. Say out loud
10. Perform
11. Not her but___
14. Possess

Down
1. Picks out
2. Opposite of goes
3. Not yes
4. Discover
5. Telling
6. Would
8. Go toward
12. Myself
13. Our Heavenly Father

Jesus answered, "My teaching is 3a.__ __ __   my own. It 2.__ __ __ __ __

4a.__ __ __ __   11.__ __ __   6a.__ __ __   7.__ __ __ __   12.__ __.

If anyone 1.__ __ __ __ __ __ __ __   8.__ __   10.__ __   God's

6d.__ __ __ __, he will 4d.__ __ __ __ out whether my

5.__ __ __ __ __ __ __ __ comes from 13.__ __ __   or whether I

9.__ __ __ __ __ __ on my 14.__ __ __."

Words of Jesus ...

In Healing

Many followed Jesus, and he
healed all their sick.
(Matthew 12:15)

Healing a Leper

Often large crowds followed Jesus, and once a man who had a bad disease came to Jesus. Find out what happened by unscrambling the letters in each box. The letters will make words to complete the story. (Matthew 8:2-3)

A 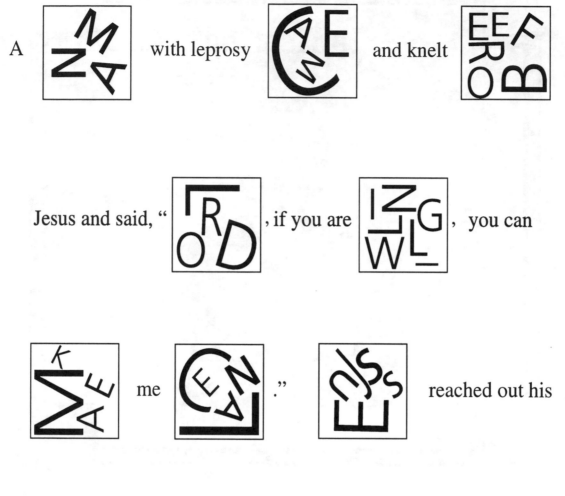 with leprosy ▢ and knelt ▢

Jesus and said, "▢, if you are ▢, you can

▢ me ▢." ▢ reached out his

 and touched the man. "I am willing," he said. "Be !"

Immediately he was ▢ of his ▢.

Healing a Blind Man in Bethsaida

In the town of Bethsaida a blind man was brought to Jesus. Jesus put his hands on the man's eyes and the man said he could see people, but they looked like trees. Jesus put his hands on the man's eyes again and the man could see everything clearly. Then Jesus told him something. Find what Jesus said by drawing a straight line to connect the trees with the same numbers. Each line will go through a word. Write the words in the blanks. (Mark 8:26, footnote a)

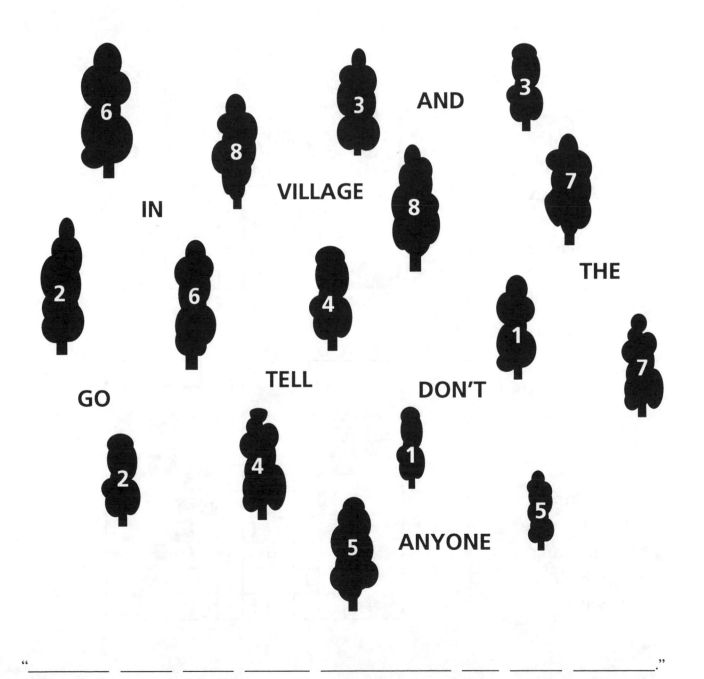

"_____ ____ ____ _____ _____ ____ _____ _____."

Healing on the Sabbath

On the Sabbath day Jesus went to the synagogue (church) to teach, and a man came to him. The man's hand was shriveled, and Jesus told the man to stand in front of everyone. Then he said to the man, "Stretch out your hand," and the man's hand was completely restored. You can read the story in Luke 6:6-10.

Below are four puzzles that use words from the Bible account. Use the word list beside each puzzle to fill in the blank squares.

"A" Words

hand

law

lawful

reason

Sabbath

stand

teaching

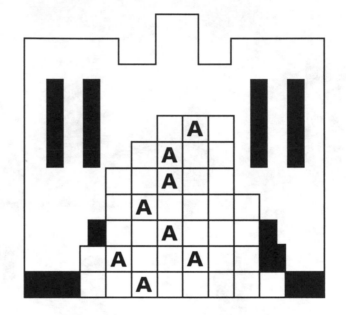

"I" Words

him

if

life

looking

Pharisees

thinking

which

with

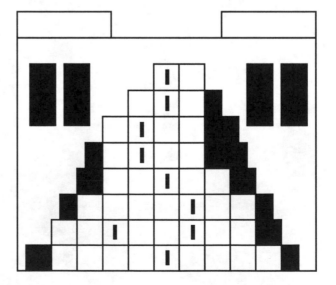

"E" Words

accuse
he
heal
Jesus
see
stretch
synagogue
teachers
watched

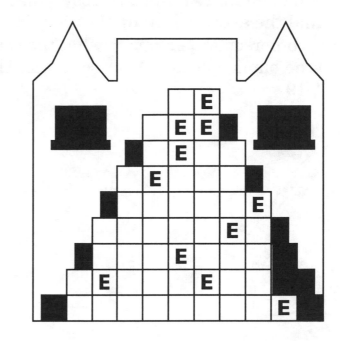

"O" Words

destroy
do
front
good
looked
restored
so
stood

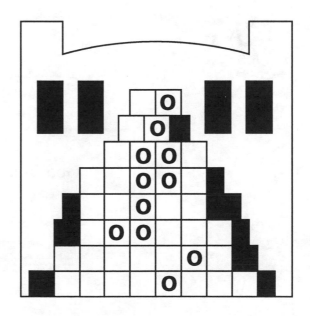

Healing Ten Men

Ten men had an illness called leprosy. What happened when they met Jesus? To find the answer, look up the story in the Bible, then draw a line from each person or persons to what they said. Copy the missing words into the blank spaces in each sentence. The story is found in Luke 17:11-19.

A.

B.

C.

1. "Go, ___ ___ ___ ___ yourselves

   to the ___ ___ ___ ___ ___ ___ ___."

2. "___ ___ ___ ___ ___ are the

   ___ ___ ___ ___ ___ nine?"

3. "Jesus, ___ ___ ___ ___ ___ ___,

   have ___ ___ ___ ___ on us."

4. One of them ___ ___ ___ ___ back,

   ___ ___ ___ ___ ___ ___ ___ ___

   God in a ___ ___ ___ ___

   ___ ___ ___ ___ ___.

5. "___ ___ ___ ___ and go;

   your ___ ___ ___ ___ ___

   has made you ___ ___ ___ ___."

28

Healing a Man's Ear

Fit the words into the squares, then into the story, matching the numbers. The story is found in Luke 22: 49-52.

Jesus 6._____ to his 10._____ Father in the Garden of Gethsemane. He knew the soldiers were coming to 2._____ him and that he was going to die for the 8._____ of all people. When the soldiers came, Jesus' followers said, "Lord, should we 7._____ with our swords?" One of them struck the 5._____ of the high priest and 9._____ off his 4._____.

Jesus said, "3._____ more of this!" And he touched the 11._____ ear and 1a._____ him. He said to the soldiers, "This is your 1d._____ when darkness reigns." Then Jesus was crucified for our sins. But he rose again, completely healed.

Word list

arrest
cut
ear
healed
heavenly
hour
man's
no
prayed
servant
sins
strike

Healing a Blind Man in Jericho

To find out about a man who asked Jesus to heal him, follow the arrows, beginning at "Start." Copy the words in each circle to complete each sentence, then read the story. (Luke 18:35-43)

1. As Jesus approached Jericho, a blind man was _____

_____

2. When he heard the crowd going by, _____

_____

3. They told him, _____

_____

4. He called out, _____

_____

5. Those who led the way _____

_____

6. but he shouted all the more, _____

_____

7. Jesus stopped and _____

_____

8. When he came near, Jesus asked him, _____

_____

9. "Lord, _____

_____

10. Jesus said to him, _____

_____

11. Immediately he _____

_____

12. When all the people _____

_____

START

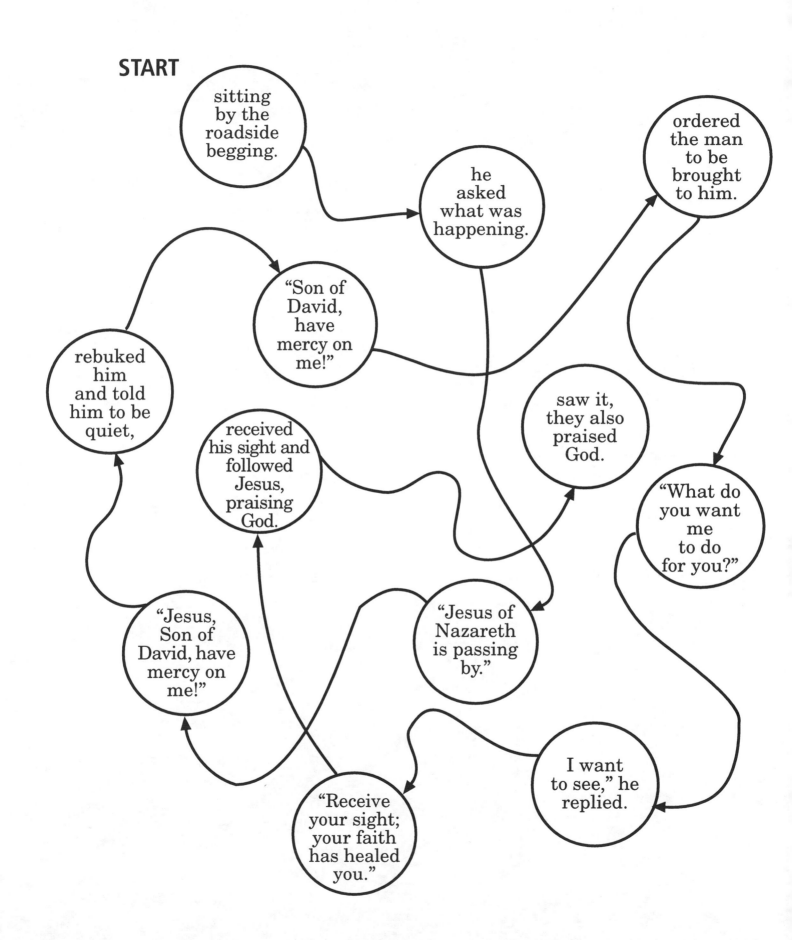

sitting by the roadside begging.

he asked what was happening.

ordered the man to be brought to him.

"Son of David, have mercy on me!"

rebuked him and told him to be quiet,

received his sight and followed Jesus, praising God.

saw it, they also praised God.

"What do you want me to do for you?"

"Jesus, Son of David, have mercy on me!"

"Jesus of Nazareth is passing by."

I want to see," he replied.

"Receive your sight; your faith has healed you."

Words of Jesus ...

In Miracles

A miracle is something that happens that cannot be explained. Jesus did many miracles because he is the Son of God and has the power of God.

"All authority in heaven and on earth has been given to me."

(Matthew 28:18)

A Miracle at Cana

Read the story of Jesus' first miracle in John 2:1-11. Then answer the questions and place the answers in the blanks. The letters in the boxes will spell something.

1. There were stone water _____ v.6

2. What ceremony took place? _____ v.1

3. "You have saved the _____ ." v.10

4. "Do whatever he tells _____ ." v.5

5. Who first tasted the new wine?_____ v.9

6. " _____ the jars with water." v.7

7. How many jars were there? _____ v.6

8. What did Jesus reveal? _____ v.11

9. "You have _____ the best." v.10

10. "My _____ has not yet come." v.4

11. Jesus said, "Dear _____ ." v.4

12. On the _____ day v.1

13. This was Jesus' _____ miracle. v.11

14. "Now _____ some out." v.8

15. A city in Galilee _____ v.1

16. Twenty to thirty _____ v.6

17. Jesus' _____ said, "They have no more wine." v.3

34

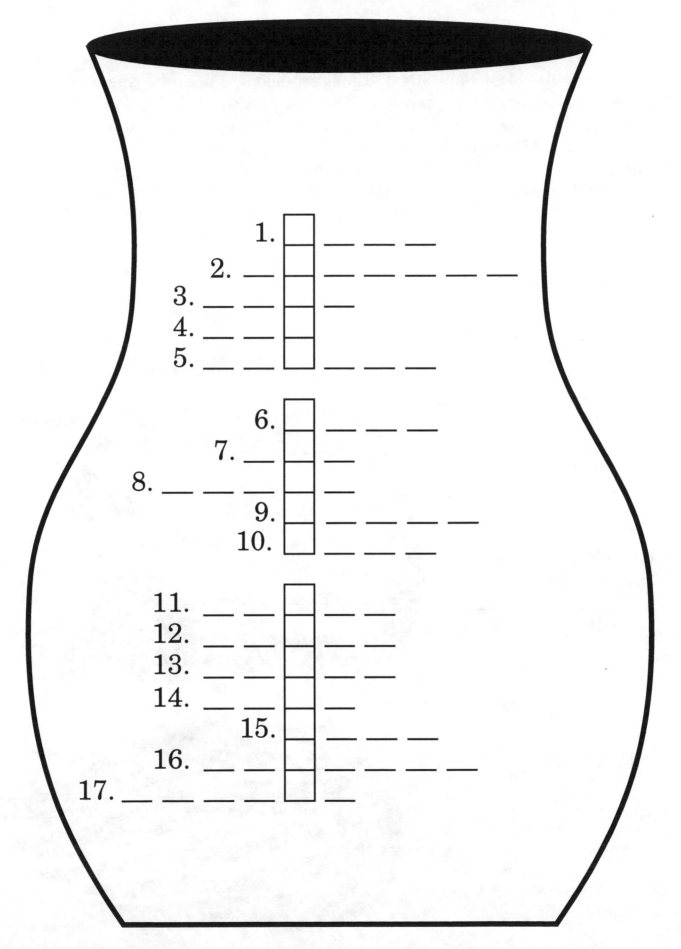

A Miracle in a Storm

One evening Jesus and his disciples crossed a lake and Jesus was asleep. Suddenly a storm came up. The disciples woke Jesus and asked, "Teacher, don't you care if we drown?" Jesus stood up and said to the waves, "Quiet! Be still!" Immediately the wind stopped blowing and the water became calm. Then Jesus asked his disciples . . .

To find what Jesus asked, write a word for each meaning given. Then place the letters in the blank squares in the boat, matching the numbers. (Mark 4:35-40)

a. It is made from trees.

___ ___ ___
1   2   3

b. You buy things at the

___ ___ ___ ___
4   5   6   7

c. 4 times 10 =

___ ___ ___ ___
8   9

d. Jesus __ me,
   this I know

___ ___ ___ ___ ___
10   11

e. Not over but

___ ___ ___ ___
12 13

f. Frozen rain is

___ ___ ___ ___
14 15 16

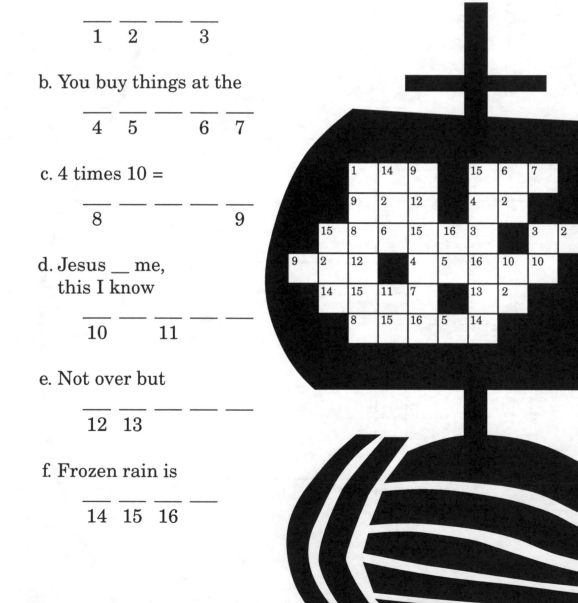

36

A Miracle of Food

A large crowd of people followed Jesus into the country to hear his teachings. At evening his disciples said, "Send the crowds away, so they can go to the villages and buy themselves some food." Jesus said, "They don't need to go away. You give them something to eat." The disciples only had a few loaves of bread and a few fish. Jesus told the people to sit down. Then he gave thanks for the food and broke the bread and fish into pieces. Everyone ate and there were basketfuls of food left over. (Matthew 14:15-21)

Work the following arithmetic problems to answer the questions and learn more.

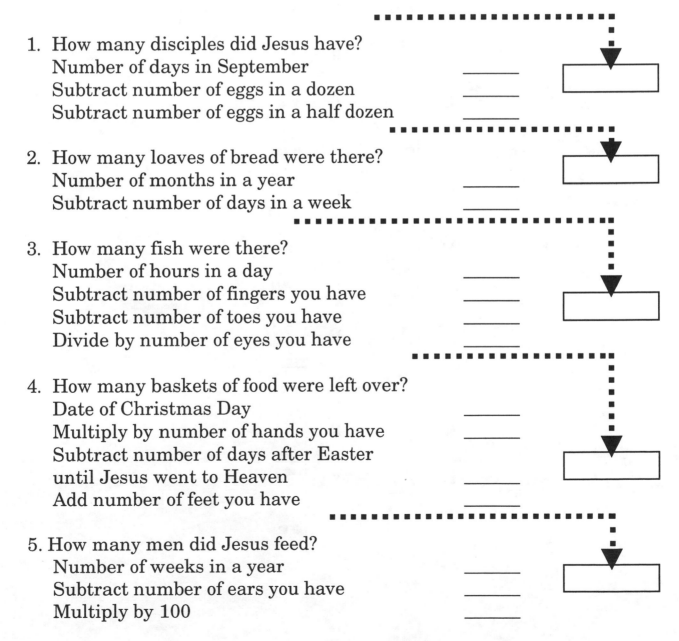

1. How many disciples did Jesus have?
   Number of days in September   _____
   Subtract number of eggs in a dozen   _____
   Subtract number of eggs in a half dozen   _____

2. How many loaves of bread were there?
   Number of months in a year   _____
   Subtract number of days in a week   _____

3. How many fish were there?
   Number of hours in a day   _____
   Subtract number of fingers you have   _____
   Subtract number of toes you have   _____
   Divide by number of eyes you have   _____

4. How many baskets of food were left over?
   Date of Christmas Day   _____
   Multiply by number of hands you have   _____
   Subtract number of days after Easter
   until Jesus went to Heaven   _____
   Add number of feet you have   _____

5. How many men did Jesus feed?
   Number of weeks in a year   _____
   Subtract number of ears you have   _____
   Multiply by 100   _____

A Miracle about Money

Some tax collectors asked Jesus' disciple, Peter, whether or not Jesus paid taxes. Jesus told Peter how to get the money to pay the tax. Use the code to find out what Jesus told Peter to do. (Matthew 17:24-27)

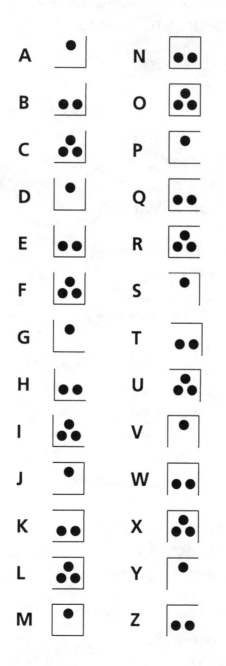

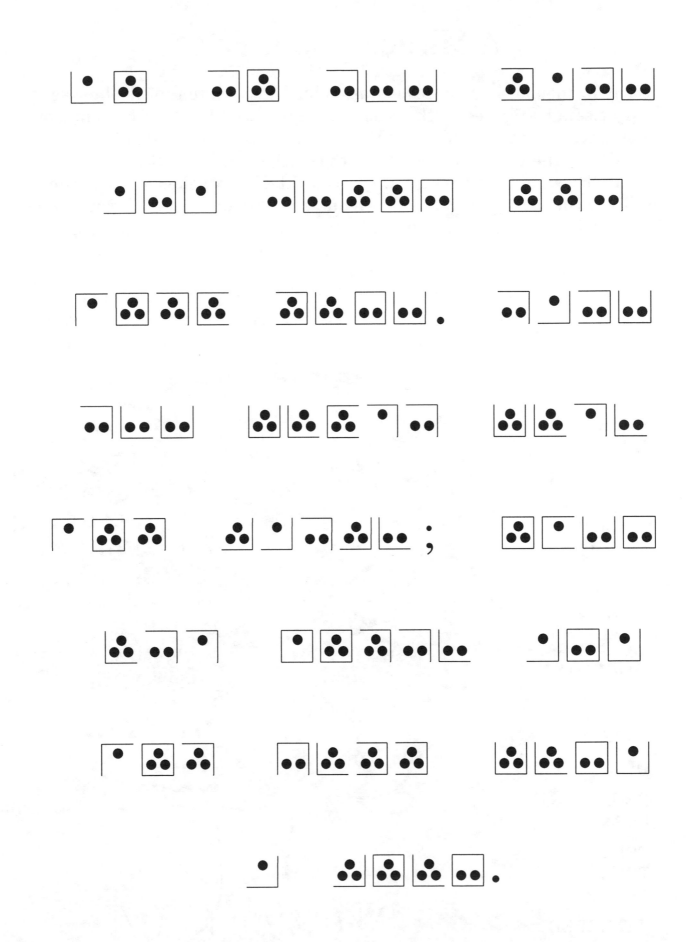

A Miracle about Fruit

Early in the morning, as Jesus was on his way back to the city, he was hungry. Seeing a fig tree by the road, he went up to it but found nothing on it except leaves. Then he said to it, "May you never bear fruit again!" Immediately the tree withered. When the disciples saw this, they were amazed. "How did the fig tree wither so quickly?" they asked. Jesus replied, "I tell you the truth, if you have faith and do not doubt, not only can you do what was done to the fig tree, but also you can say to this mountain, 'Go, throw yourself into the sea,' and it will be done. If you believe, you will receive whatever you ask for in prayer." (Matthew 21:18-22)

The words in the word list are taken from the story. Find them in the puzzle. Words may be diagonal, vertical or horizontal, backward or forward.

BEAR
BELIEVE

DISCIPLES
DOUBT

FAITH
FRUIT

HUNGRY

LEAVES

MORNING
MOUNTAIN

NOTHING

PRAYER

QUICKLY

RECEIVE
ROAD

TELL
TREE
TRUTH

WITHERED

```
F A I T H B M N C T S B M
O D P R E Q O F R E G E Q
L T H U N G R Y L L S L U
E I H T U E N P I L R I I
A U V H Y J I O W K E E C
V R X A L C N Y T M C V K
E F R Z S N G B O H E E L
S P C I D E R E H T I W Y
  S D O U B T R D F V N R
  M O U N T A I N E G G
    S H T O E J V K
    E E R T B W L Y
```

40

The Greatest Miracle

Read John 20:19-23. Then change one letter in each of the underlined words in the following sentences so that the sentence makes sense.

1. When the disciples were together
   with the doors <u>looked</u>   _____
2. for fear of the <u>pews</u>,   _____
3. Jesus came and <u>stool</u> among them.   _____
4. He said, "<u>Peach</u> be with you."   _____
5. Then he showed them his <u>bands</u>   _____
6. And his <u>ride</u>.   _____
7. Again he said, "<u>Place</u> be with you.   _____
8. As the Father has <u>cent</u> me,   _____
9. I am <u>rending</u> you."   _____
10. Then he breathed on them and <u>maid</u>,   _____
11. "<u>Releive</u> the Holy Spirit.   _____
12. If you forgive anyone his <u>tins</u>,   _____
13. they are <u>forliven</u>.   _____
14. If you do <u>hot</u> forgive them,   _____
15. they are <u>lot</u> forgiven."   _____

Fit the underlined words into the cross.
   <u>When</u> Jesus <u>rose</u> <u>from</u> the <u>dead</u>, <u>it</u> was the greatest miracle of <u>all</u>.

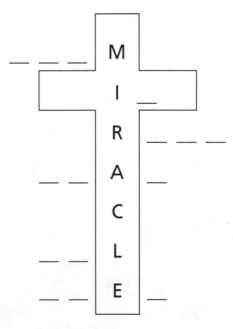

41

Words of Jesus ...

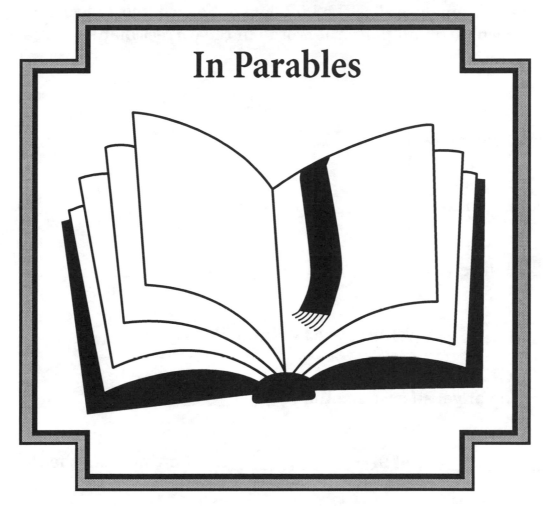

In Parables

A parable is an earthly story with a heavenly meaning. The Bible says: "With many similar parables Jesus spoke the word to [the people], as much as they could understand. He did not say anything to them without using a parable. But when he was alone with his own disciples, he explained everything." (Mark 4:33-34)

A Parable about Heaven

What is the kingdom of heaven like? Jesus told the people that it is like a mustard seed, which a man planted in his garden. It grew and became a tree, and the birds of the air perched in its branches. (Matthew 13:31) The book of Revelation describes the kingdom of heaven, too. Unscramble the letters in each bird and place the words in the correct blanks to read more about heaven.

"[The angel] showed me the 1._____ 2._____,

Jerusalem, coming 3._____ out of 4._____ from God.

. . . Its brilliance was like that of a very precious 5._____ . . .

6._____ as crystal." (Revelation 21:10-11)

"Then the angel showed me the 7._____ of the

8._____ of 9._____ . . . flowing from the throne of

God and of the 10._____." (Revelation 22:1)

"On each side of the river stood the 11._____ of life, bear-

ing twelve crops of 12._____." (Revelation 22:2)

A Parable about Treasures

Jesus told a parable about two men who found special treasure. Read the story in Matthew 13:44-46. All of the words in the crossword puzzle—except one—can be found in the Bible verses. Which word in the puzzle is not in the Bible story?

ACROSS
1. Paid money for
3. Owned
4. Departed
6. The same as
9. Jesus lives in
10. Fantastic!
11. Opposite of lost
12. Adam was the first
13. Large grassy area

DOWN
2. Three minus two
3. Opposite of she
4. At what time?
5. Something valuable
6. Jesus ____s me
7. A king rules his ____
8. A kind of jewel

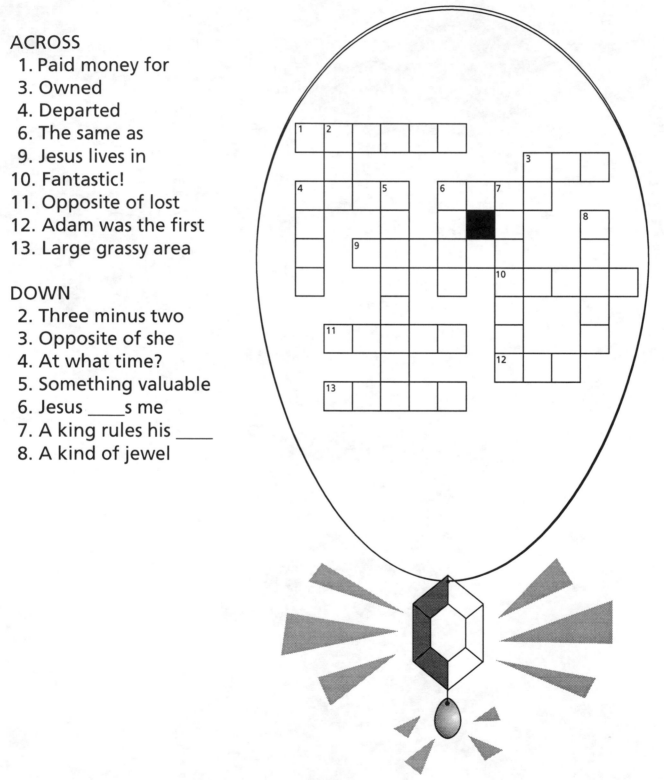

A Parable about Neighbors

Jesus said we should love our neighbor, and he told a parable to show us who our neighbor is. (Luke 10:30-37) A man was traveling from Jerusalem to Jericho. Robbers attacked him, beat him and took his clothes. A priest passed by and also a Levite, but they did not help the man. A Samaritan saw the man and bandaged his wounds. Then he helped the man rise up. He put the man on his donkey, took him to an inn and paid the innkeeper to care for the wounded man. Jesus wants us to love our neighbors and said everyone is our neighbor. Use the clues to fill in the puzzle squares. The last letter of each word is the first letter of the next word. Now answer the question, "Who is your neighbor?"

CLUES

1. A _____ passed by
2. ____ he helped the man
3. Who our _____ is
4. _____ attacked him
5. to _____us who
6. bandaged his _____
7. A _____ saw the man

8. they did _____ help the man
9. he _____ a parable
10. they _____ not help
11. put the man on his _____
12. Who is _____ neighbor?
13. he helped the man _____ _____
14. Jesus told many _____

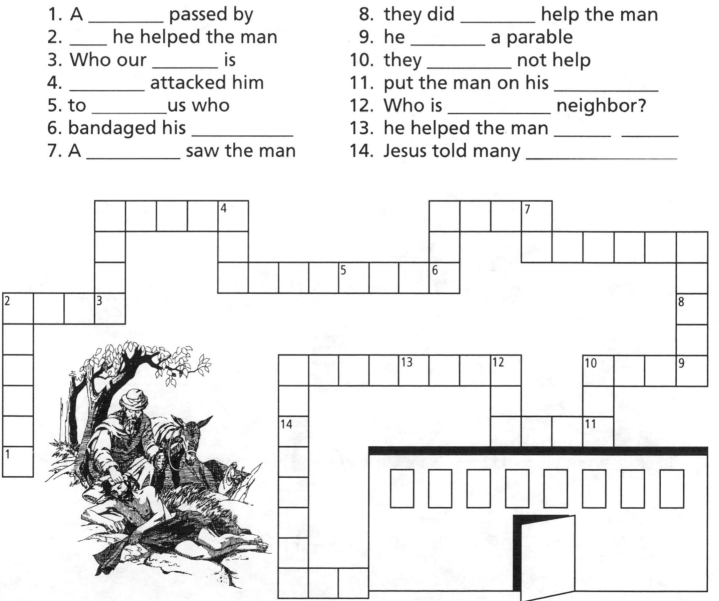

Lost and Found

A woman had 1._____ 2._____ and lost one. She lit a 3._____, swept the 4._____, and searched until she found the coin. Then she called her friends and said, "Be 5._____ with me, for I found the coin." Jesus said, "In the same way, the 6._____ of God rejoice over one sinner who repents." (Luke 15:8-10)

Spell the name of the things pictured below. Add and subtract the letters and place each answer in the correct blanks to read about what was found.

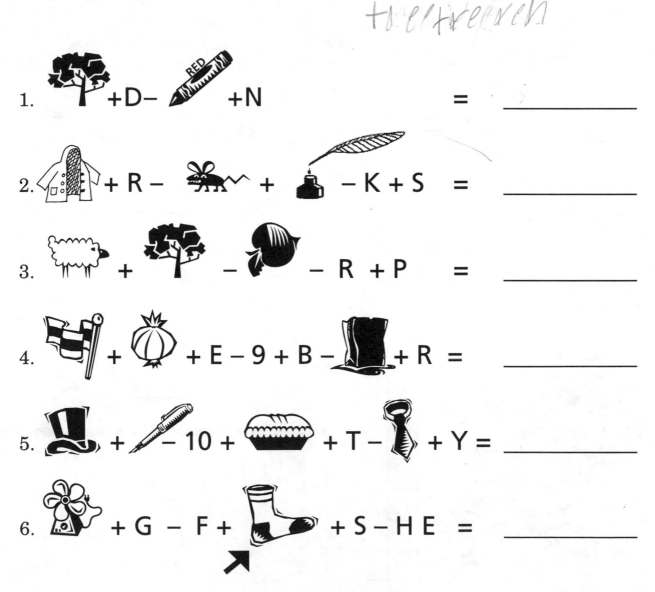

1. [tree] +D– [crayon RED] +N = _____

2. [coat] + R – [mouse] + [quill/inkwell] – K + S = _____

3. [sheep] + [tree] – [onion] – R +P = _____

4. [flag] + [onion] + E – 9 + B – [hat] + R = _____

5. [hat] + [pen] – 10 + [bread] + T – [tie] + Y = _____

6. [pinwheel] + G – F+ [sock] + S – H E = _____

A Parable about a Rich Man

Jesus told this parable: "The ground of a certain rich man produced a good crop. He thought to himself, 'What shall I do? I have no place to store my crops.' Then he said, 'This is what I'll do. I will tear down my barns and build bigger ones, and there I will store all my grain and my goods. And I'll say to myself, "You have plenty of good things laid up for many years. Take life easy; eat, drink and be merry."' But God said to him, 'You fool! This very night your life will be demanded from you. Then who will get what you have prepared for yourself?'" (Luke 12:16-20)

The words in the Word List are found in the story. Fit those words into the squares.

Word List
barns
bigger
build
certain
demanded
drink
eat
for
grain
ground
life
night
ones
prepared
rich
who

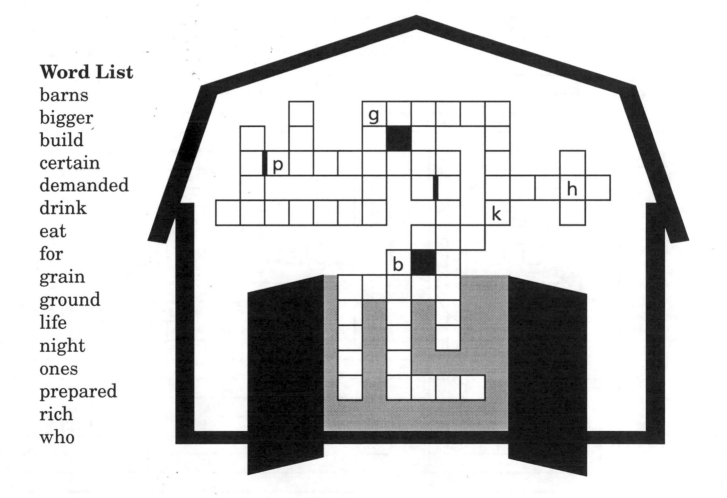

A Parable about Prayer

How should we pray? Jesus told a parable about two men. One was a Pharisee who prayed about what a good man he thought he was. The other man, a tax collector, bowed his head and said, "God have mercy on me, a sinner." Jesus said the tax collector was a humble man who was justified before God. (Luke 18:10-14)

Find the Pharisee's path to the temple. Find the tax collector's path to his home.

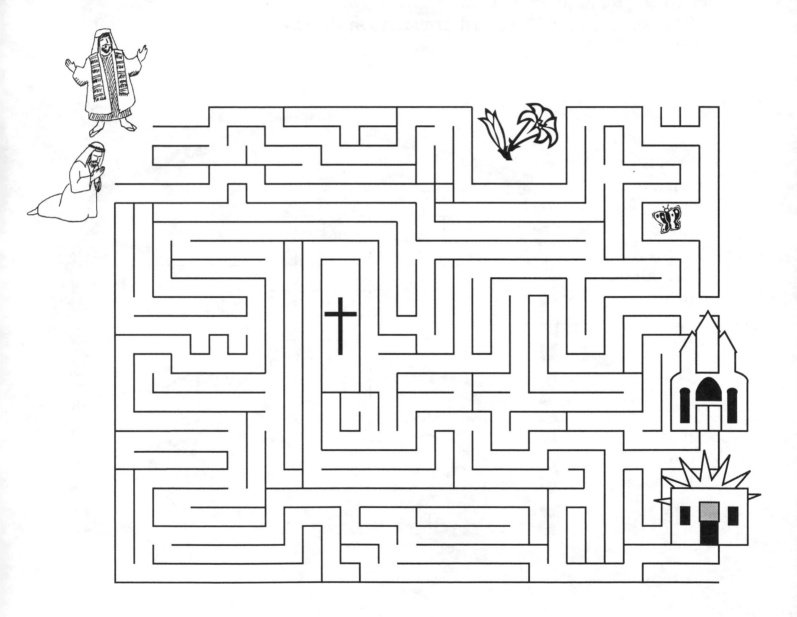

Words of Jesus ...

In Blessings

Now when [Jesus] saw the crowds, he went up on a mountainside and sat down. His disciples came to him, and he began to teach them, saying, "Blessed . . . ."

(Matthew 5:1-2)

The Beatitudes

When Jesus preached on the mountainside, he began by talking about blessings. Those blessings are called the Beatitudes. The first one tells us that we can look to Jesus for everything we need. (Matthew 5:3)

To read the first Beatitude, use the code below.

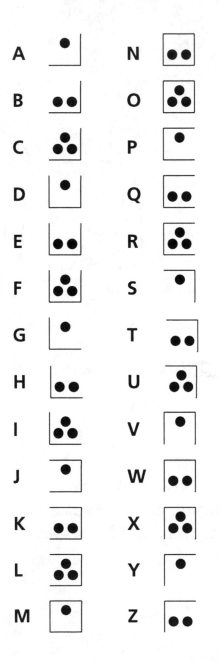

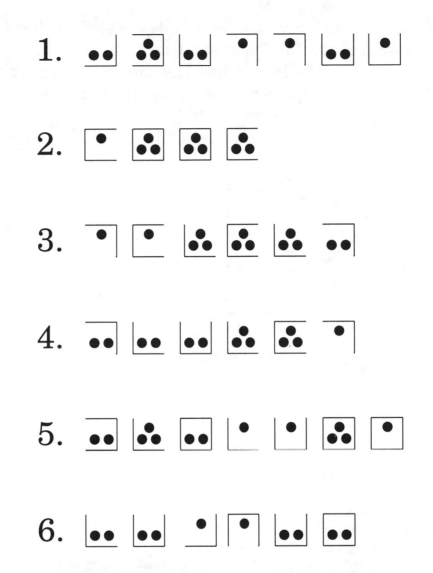

1. _____ are the 2. _____

in 3. _____, for 4._____

is the 5. _____ of 6. _____.

Help When You Are Sad

We are sad when someone we know dies. Jesus told us that God is always with us and will comfort us in sad times.

Use the word list to fit the letters into the squares. Then write the words in the Bible, matching the numbers, and read the second Beatitude. (Matthew 5:4)

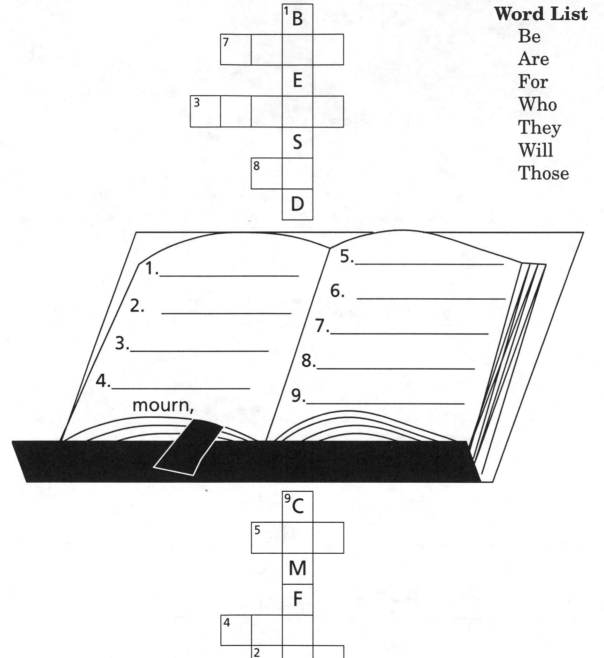

Word List
Be
Are
For
Who
They
Will
Those

1. _____
2. _____
3. _____
4. _____
mourn,
5. _____
6. _____
7. _____
8. _____
9. _____

Being Kind

When someone calls you bad names, do you want to call them bad names too? This Beatitude tells you why you should be kind. (Matthew 5:5)

Fill in the words in the word list to read the Beatitude. Transfer the letters to the blanks by matching the numbers. No number can be used twice.

Definition

1. You chew with them

2. Part of your foot

3. Dripping water

4. A charge for overdue library books

5. Perhaps

6. What a cowboy rides

7. A need for water

8. Had in your hand

9. An author is a _____.

Word List

__ __ __ __ __
35 3 15 21 37

__ __ __ __
12 6 39 27

__ __ __ __
2 32 8 17

__ __ __ __
18 26 30 38

__ __ __ __ __
14 40 24 1 10

__ __ __ __ __
43 19 33 5 23

__ __ __ __ __ __
42 22 29 9 4 36

__ __ __ __
31 13 28 7

__ __ __ __ __ __
25 20 34 11 16 41

__ __ __ __ __ __ __
1 2 3 4 5 6 7

__ __ __ __ __ __
8 9 10   11 12 13

__ __ __ __ , __ __ __
14 15 16 17   18 19 20

__ __ __ __ __ __ __ __
21 22 23 24 25 26 27 28

__ __ __ __ __ __ __
29 30 31 32 33 34 35

__ __ __ __ __ __ __ __
36 37 38   39 40 41 42 43

A Promise

This Beatitude tells you to be hungry and thirsty for something. To find out what that is, follow the arrows and place each letter in the blank space in the order in which you find them. (Matthew 5:6)

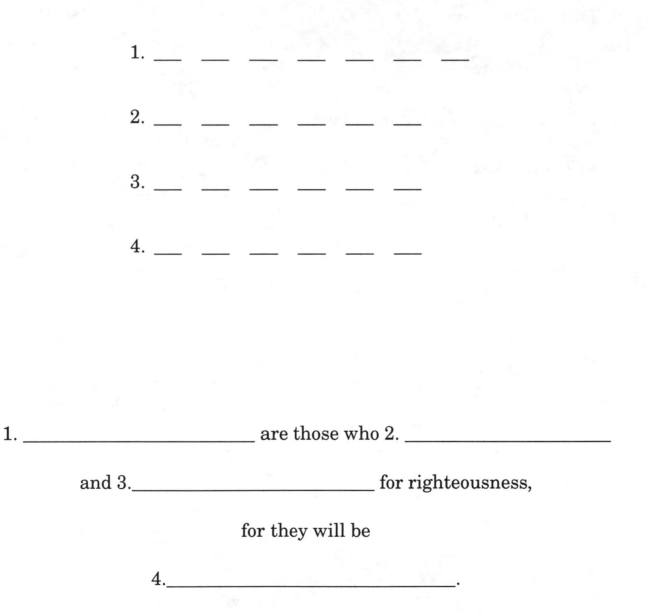

1. __ __ __ __ __ __ __

2. __ __ __ __ __ __

3. __ __ __ __ __ __

4. __ __ __ __ __ __

1. _____ are those who 2. _____

and 3._____ for righteousness,

for they will be

4._____.

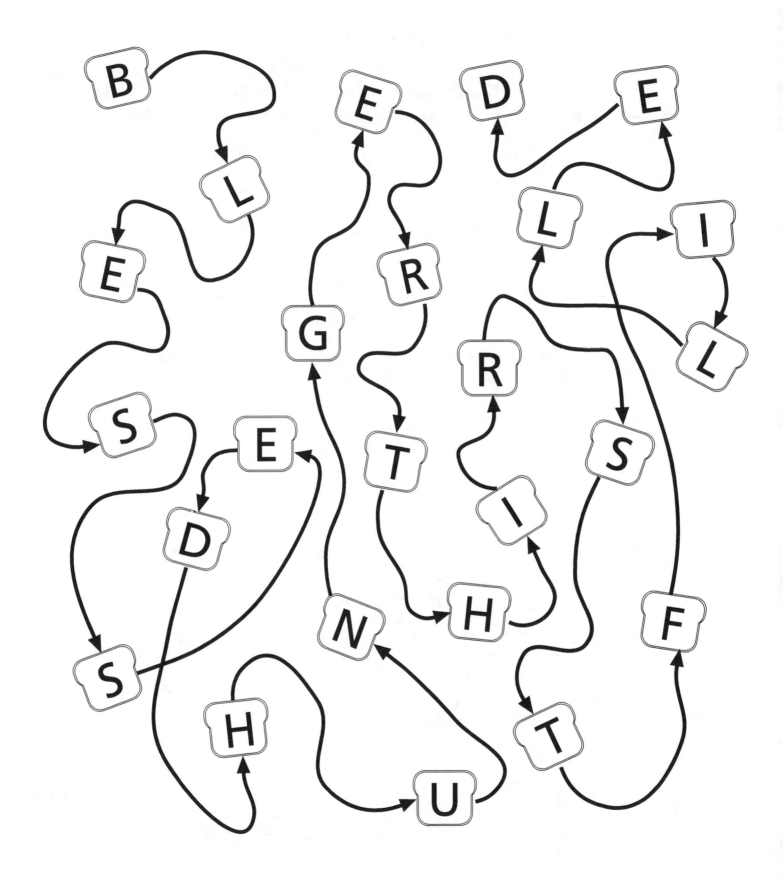

Showing Mercy

The fifth Beatitude is: "Blessed are the merciful, for they will be shown mercy" (Matthew 5:7). How can we show mercy? How will that make us feel?

Find the missing words in the sentence by matching the numbers and placing the letters into the blanks.

If we are __ __ __ __ ,   __ __ __ __ __ __ __ ,   __ __ __ __ __ __ __
        1 2 3 4   5 6 7 8 9 10 11   12 13 14 15 16 17 18

and __ __ __ __ __ __   then we will be __ __ __ __ __   and
     19 20 21 22 23 24   25 26 27 28 29

__ __ __ __ __ __   and we will __ __ __ __ __ __   __ __ __ .
30 31 32 33 34 35   36 37 38 39 40 41   42 43 44

P 8 G 24 D 4 T 18 I 39

V 21 T 14 J 30 H 5 U 34

K 1 A 38 N 17 O 31 L 11 S 40 A 26

P 27 F 33 E 6 Y 29 O 43 F 9 I 22

A 13 G 42 L 19 R 37 I 2 P 28 E 16

H 25 D 44 U 10 Y 32 N 23 P 36 L 7

N 3 L 35 O 20 P 12 E 41 I 15

58

Holding On to Good Thoughts

Fill in the blanks in this Beatitude by adding and subtracting letters using the plus and minus signs. (Matthew 5:8)

Blessed are the 1. _ _ _ _ in 2. _ _ _ _ _,

for they will   3. _ _ _   4. _ _ _.

– M P K I N +   – T E =   1. _____

– E L +   – D   = 2. _____

6 – I X +   – N E D L   = 3. _____

– A T E +   – W O   = 4. _____

Words of Peace

Jesus said, "Blessed are the peacemakers, for they will be called children of God. (Matthew 5:9, NRSV) Jesus wants us to have peace and be peacemakers.

Below are some Bible verses about peace. Write in order all of the letters in the number "1" squares, then number "2," etc., to complete the verse.

1. Jesus told his disciples to "be at peace __ __ __ __   __ __ __ __
                                                   1 1 1 1   1 1 1 1

    __ __ __ __ __ . " (Mark 9:50)
    1 1 1 1 1

2. The priest, Zechariah, asked God to "guide our __ __ __ __
                                                           2 2 2 2

    __ __ __ __ the __ __ __ __ of peace." (Luke 1:79)
    2 2 2 2   2 2 2 2

3. When Jesus was born, angels sang, "Glory to God in the highest

    __ __ __ __ __ __ __ __ __ __ peace to __ __ __." (Luke 2:14)
    3 3 3   3 3   3 3 3 3 3   3 3 3

4. On Palm Sunday the people sang joyfully, "Peace in __ __ __ __ __ __
                                                                  4 4 4 4 4 4

    and glory in the __ __ __ __ __ __ __." (Luke 19:38)
                        4 4 4 4 4 4 4

5. The disciples were together when suddenly Jesus appeared and said,

    " __ __ __ __ __ __ __ __ __ __ __ you." (Luke 24:36)
      5 5 5 5 5   5 5   5 5 5 5

¹W	²F	³A	⁴H	⁵P	¹I	²E	³N	⁴E	⁵E	¹T
²E	³D	⁴A	⁵A	¹H	²T	³O	⁴V	⁵C	¹E	²I
³N	⁴E	⁵E	¹A				²N	³E	⁴N	⁵B
¹C	²T					³A	⁴H	⁵E	¹H	
²O	³R							⁴I	⁵W	
¹O	²P	³T						⁴G	⁵I	
¹T	²A	³H	⁴H					⁵T	¹H	
²T	³M	⁴E	⁵E	¹H	²E	³H	⁴E	¹S	³R	⁴N	⁴T

Blessing in Persecution

Did anyone ever make fun of you for something you believe? That is what "persecuted" means. Work the puzzle to read another Beatitude.

Use each clue to write a five-letter word in Column 1. Use another clue to write a four-letter word in Column 2, using letters in Column 1. Place the leftover letter in Column 3. The words in Column 3 will complete the Beatitude below.

"Blessed are those who are persecuted because of righteousness, for theirs is the _____ of _____." (Matthew 5:10)

CLUES

1. Smash into pieces
2. A toy teddy _____
3. Rubber part of a car's wheels
4. Take a nap
5. At no time
6. All the time
7. "How _____ Thou Art"
8. Water from your eye
9. Pour water down the _____
10. Water from heaven
11. Bend over
12. Opposite of go
13. Boiling water lets off _____
14. Chair

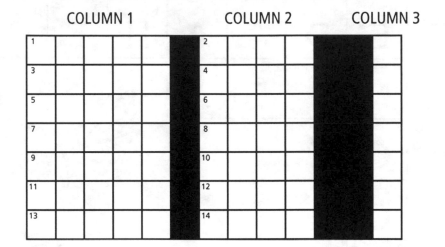

COLUMN 1   COLUMN 2   COLUMN 3

1. Not these, but _____
2. You have five on each foot
3. Beauty and the _____
4. Small flying mammals
5. Baseball groups
6. Part of a flower
7. Holders for flowers
8. Oceans
9. Jesus _____ for you
10. We ride in _____
11. A king wears it on his head
12. A kind of blackbird

COLUMN 1   COLUMN 2   COLUMN 3

Another Blessing for You

When things go wrong and you have a bad day, remember that Jesus promises you another blessing: "Blessed are you when people insult you, persecute you and falsely say all kinds of evil against you because of me." (Matthew 5:11) All of the words in this Beatitude can be found in the puzzle square. Circle each word as you find it. All words are horizontal or vertical.

```
M  A  W  M  B  O  C  P  D  Q  J
E  R  H  O  F  G  S  M  F  T  P
H  B  E  C  A  U  S  E  U  B  H
J  V  N  K  L  W  L  X  M  L  Q
Y  P  E  R  S  E  C  U  T  E  J
A  Z  Y  B  E  M  Y  A  C  S  R
P  E  O  P  L  E  O  G  N  S  K
D  V  U  S  Y  O  U  A  R  E  S
O  I  E  A  P  F  K  I  N  D  S
A  L  L  Y  O  U  G  N  Q  H  R
N  I  S  J  F  I  N  S  U  L  T
D  T  K  U  L  V  M  T  X  N  Y
```

A Joyful Blessing for You

Place the words in each pyramid by using the list of words above it. Then write the words into the sentence by matching the numbers. This is the last verse of the Beatitudes. (Matthew 5:12)

"A" Words

and	heaven
way	reward
glad	because
same	

"E" Words

be	were
the	great
the	persecuted
they	

"I" Words

is
in
in
rejoice

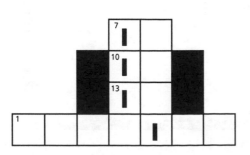

"O" Words

for
who
you
your
before
prophets

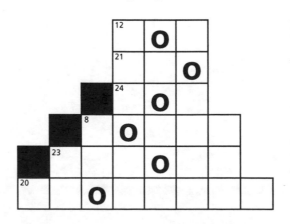

$$\overline{\hspace{3cm}}\ \ \overline{\hspace{1cm}}\ \ \overline{\hspace{0.7cm}}\ \ \overline{\hspace{1cm}}\ ,$$

1   2   3   4

5   6   7

8   9   10   11

12   13   14   15   16

17   18   19   20

21   22   23   24

ANSWERS

Page 8-9

1. room, close, door, Father, Father, reward
2. told, disciples, they, should, always, give, up
3. watch, will, fall, temptation, spirit, willing, body, weak
4. whatever, name, bring, glory, Father, ask, anything, name, will

Page 10

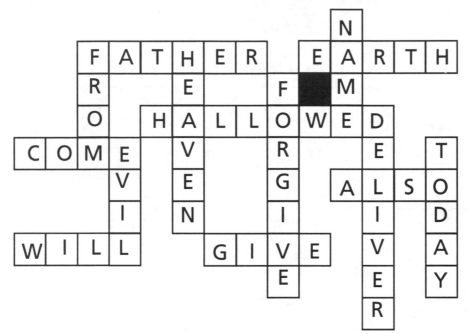

Page 11

Page 12

Father, the time has come. Glorify your Son, that your Son may glorify you. For you granted him authority over all people that he might give eternal life to all those you have given him. Now this is eternal life: that they may know you, the only true God, and Jesus Christ, whom you have sent. I have brought you glory on earth by completing the work you gave me to do. And now, Father, glorify me in your presence with the glory I had with you before the world began.

Page 13

Page 14

    a. food
    b. never
    c. thirty
    d. wheat
    e. wake
    f. tooth
    g. night
    h. ready
    i. form
    j. hen
    k. fog

Father, forgive them, for they do not know what they are doing.

Page 16

Jesus went throughout Galilee, teaching in their synagogues, preaching the good news of the kingdom, and healing every disease and sickness among the people.

Page 17

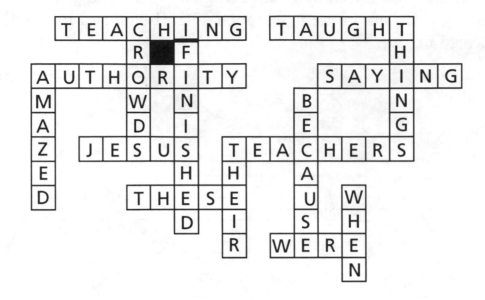

Page 18

oil – OL = I
lamp – LP = am
sheep – E + heart – AT + D = shepherd
ladybug – DBUG + S = lays
lid – D + five – IV = life
shell – LL + E + pin – IN = sheep

I am the good shepherd. The good shepherd lays down his life for the sheep.

Page 19

For God so loved the world that he gave his one and only Son, that whoever believes in him shall not perish but have eternal life.

Page 20-21

authority, disciples, baptizing, teaching, commanded, always

Page 22

My teaching is not my own. It comes from him who sent me. If anyone chooses to do God's will, he will find out whether my teaching comes from God or whether I speak on my own.

Page 24

A man with leprosy came and knelt before Jesus and said, "Lord, if you are willing you can make me clean." Jesus reached out his hand and touched the man. "I am willing," he said. "Be clean!" Immediately he was cured of his leprosy.

Page 25

"Don't go and tell anyone in the village."

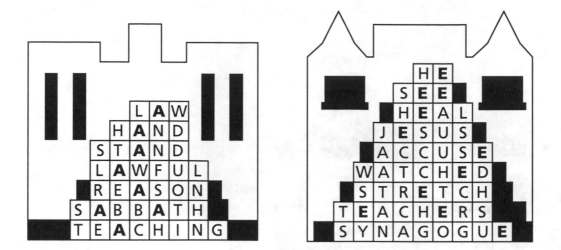

Page 28

1. a	1. show, priests
2. a	2. where, other
3. b	3. Master, pity
4. c	4. came, praising, loud, voice
5. a	5. Rise, faith, well

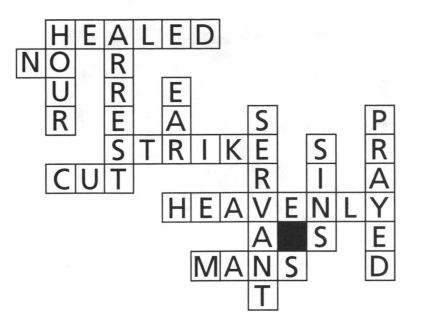

Jesus <u>prayed</u> to his <u>heavenly</u> Father in the Garden of Gethsemane. He knew the soldiers were coming to <u>arrest</u> him and that he was going to die for the <u>sins</u> of all people. When the soldiers came, Jesus' followers said, "Lord, should we <u>strike</u> with our swords?" One of them struck the <u>servant</u> of the high priest and <u>cut</u> off his <u>ear</u>.

Jesus said, "<u>No</u> more of this!" And he touched the <u>man's</u> ear and <u>healed</u> him. He said to the soldiers, "This is your <u>hour</u> when darkness reigns." Then Jesus was crucified for our sins. But he rose again, completely healed.

Page 30

1. sitting by the roadside begging.
2. he asked what was happening.
3. "Jesus of Nazareth is passing by."
4. "Jesus, Son of David, have mercy on me!"
5. rebuked him and told him to be quiet,
6. "Son of David, have mercy on me!"
7. ordered the man to be brought to him.
8. "What do you want me to do for you?"
9. I want to see," he replied.
10. "Receive your sight; your faith has healed you."
11. received his sight and followed Jesus, praising God.
12. saw it, they also praised God.

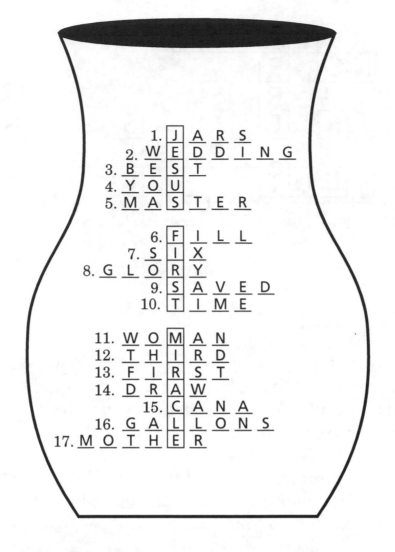

1. J A R S
2. W E D D I N G
3. B E S T
4. Y O U
5. M A S T E R

6. F I L L
7. S I X
8. G L O R Y
9. S A V E D
10. T I M E

11. W O M A N
12. T H I R D
13. F I R S T
14. D R A W
15. C A N A
16. G A L L O N S
17. M O T H E R

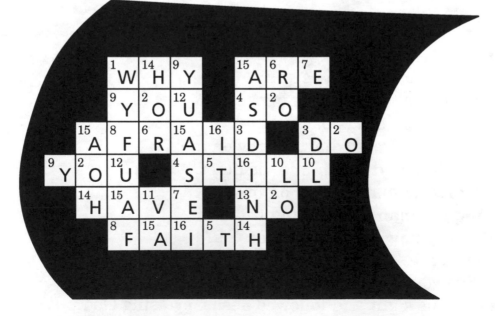

a. wood **b.** store **c.** forty **d.** loves **e.** under **f.** hail

Why are you so afraid? Do you still have no faith?

Page 37

1. 30 - 12 - 6 = 12
2. 12 - 7 = 5
3. 24 -10 - 10 ÷ 2 = 2
4. 25 x 2 - 40 + 2 = 12
5. 52 - 2 x 100 = 5000

Page 38-39

Go to the lake and throw out your line. Take the first fish you catch; open its mouth and you will find a coin.

Page 40

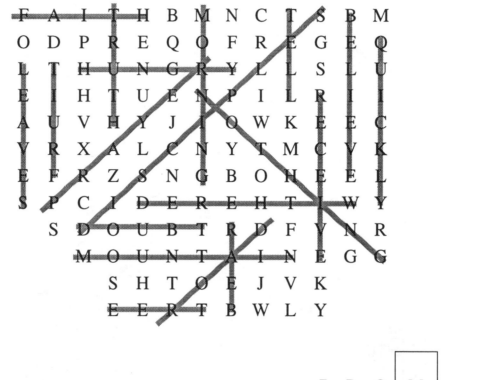

Page 41

1. locked
2. Jews
3. stood
4. Peace
5. hands
6. side
7. Peace
8. sent
9. sending
10. said
11. Receive
12. sins
13. forgiven
14. not
15. not

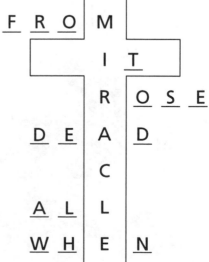

Page 44

1. holy
2. city
3. down
4. heaven
5. jewel
6. clear
7. river
8. water
9. life
10. lamb
11. tree
12. fruit

Page 46

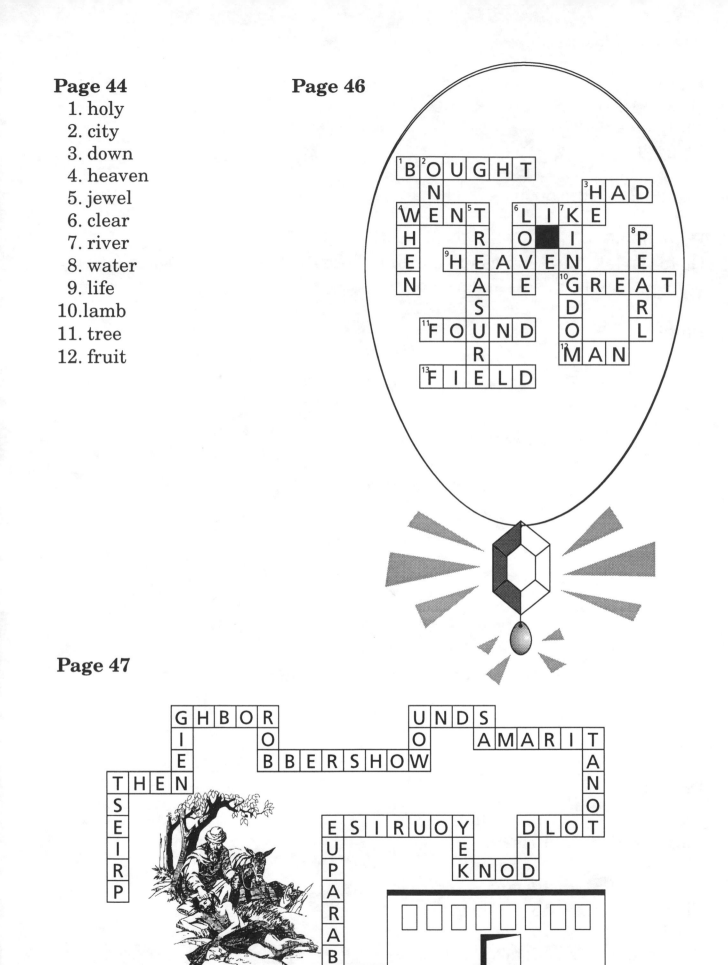

Crossword:

```
B O U G H T
N           H A D
W E N T   L I K E
H   R   O   I       P
E   H E A V E N     E
N   A   E   G R E A T
    S   D       R
  F O U N D   D O
    R         O
  F I E L D
```

Page 47

Crossword:

```
  G H B O R       U N D S
  I E       R     O   A M A R I T
  E       B B E R S H O W       A
T H E N                         N O T
S                               T
E           E S I R U O Y   D L O T
I           U       E K N O D
R           P
P           A
            R
            A
            B
            L E S
```

Page 48

1. ten
2. coins
3. lamp
4. floor
5. happy
6. angels

Page 49

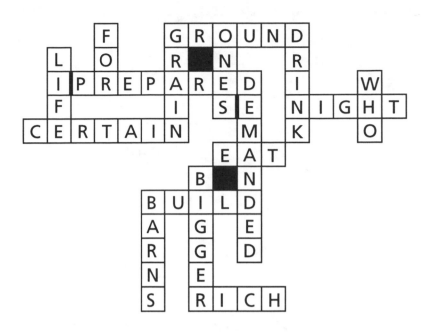

Page 50

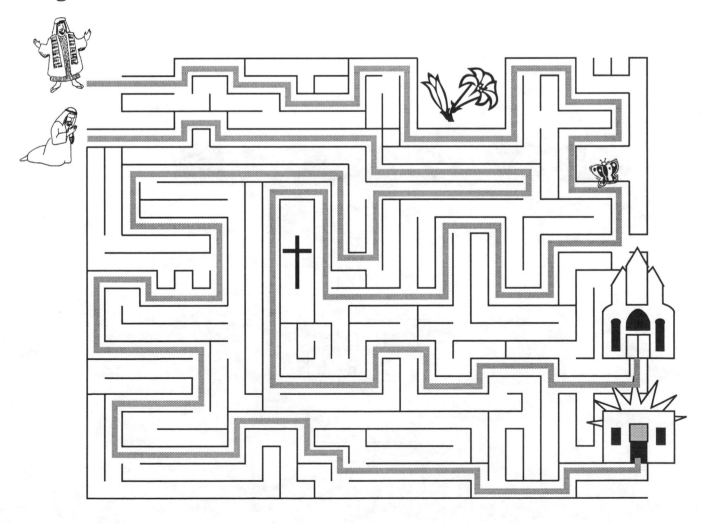

Page 52-53

Blessed are the poor in spirit, for theirs is the kingdom of heaven.

Page 54

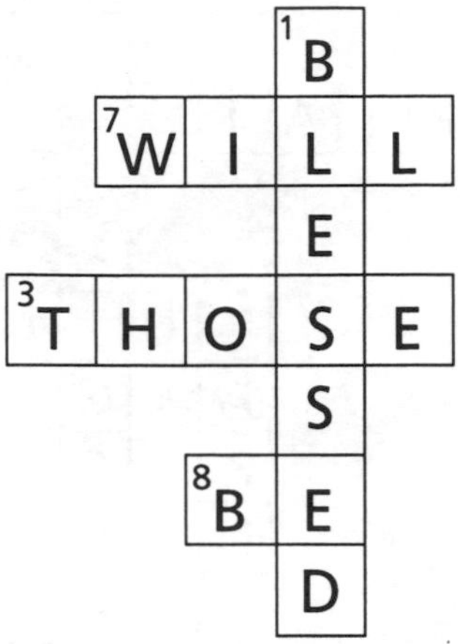
1 BLESSED
7 WILL
3 THOSE
8 BE

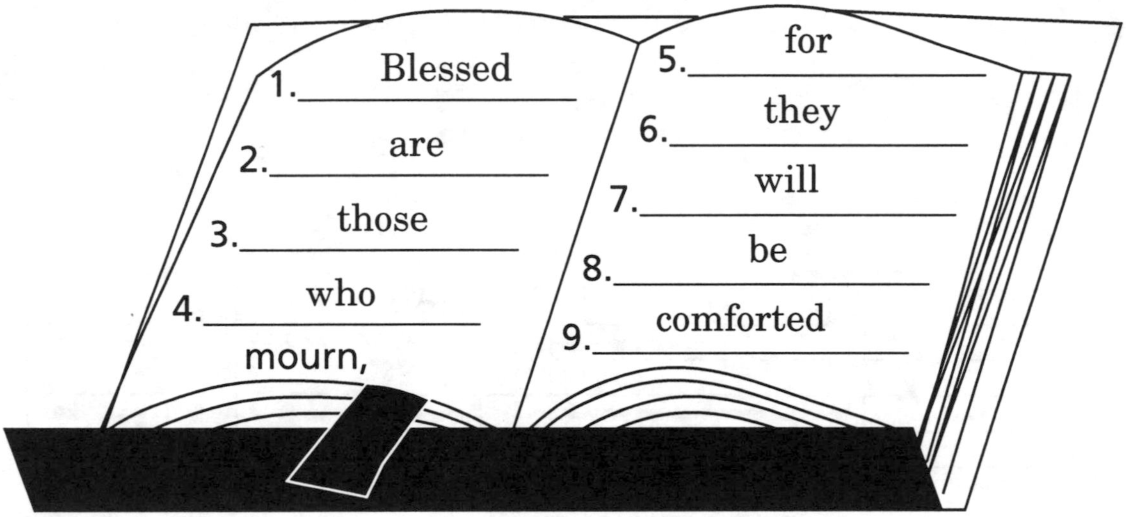
1. Blessed
2. are
3. those
4. who
mourn,
5. for
6. they
7. will
8. be
9. comforted

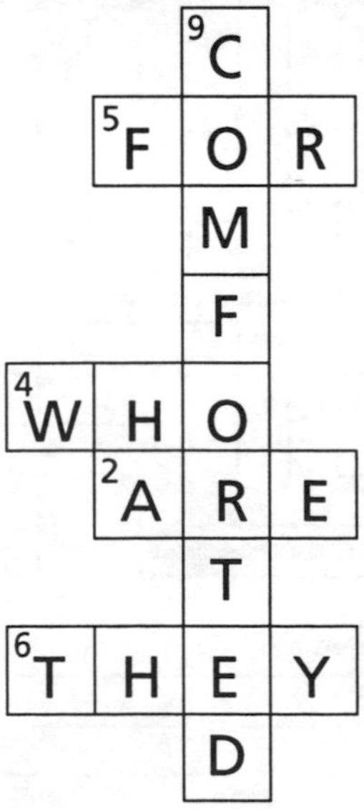
9 COMFORTED
5 FOR
4 WHO
2 ARE
6 THEY

Page 55
1. teeth
2. heel
3. leak
4. fine
5. maybe
6. horse
7. thirst
8. held
9. writer

Beatitude: Blessed are the meek, for they will inherit the earth.

Page 56-57
Blessed are those who hunger and thirst for righteousness, for they will be filled.

Page 58
kind, helpful, patient, loving, happy, joyful, praise God

Page 59
1. pure
2. heart
3. see
4. God.

Page 60
1. with each other
2. feet into . . . path
3. and on earth . . . men
4. heaven . . . highest
5. peace be with

Page 62

	COLUMN 1		COLUMN 2		COLUMN 3
1	BREAK	2	BEAR		K
3	TIRES	4	REST		I
5	NEVER	6	EVER		N
7	GREAT	8	TEAR		G
9	DRAIN	10	RAIN		D
11	STOOP	12	STOP		O
13	STEAM	14	SEAT		M

	COLUMN 1		COLUMN 2		COLUMN 3
1	THOSE	2	TOES		H
3	BEAST	4	BATS		E
5	TEAMS	6	STEM		A
7	VASES	8	SEAS		V
9	CARES	10	CARS		E
11	CROWN	12	CROW		N

Page 63

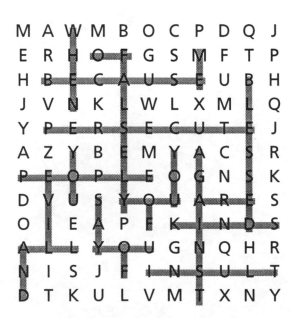

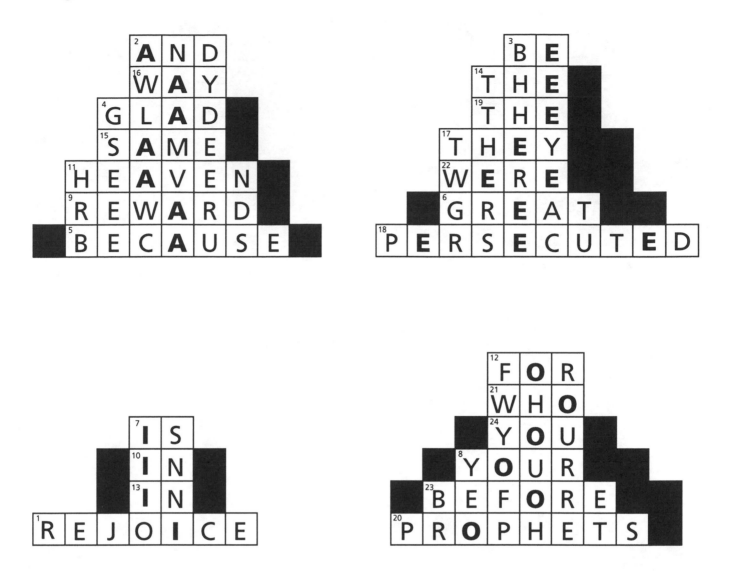

"Rejoice and be glad, because great is your reward in heaven, for in the same way they persecuted the prophets who were before you."